It's Just Sex

by Jeff Gould

A Samuel French Acting Edition

New York Hollywood London Toronto

SAMUELFRENCH.COM

Copyright © 2011 by Jeff Gould

ALL RIGHTS RESERVED

CAUTION: Professionals and amateurs are hereby warned that *IT'S JUST SEX* is subject to a licensing fee. It is fully protected under the copyright laws of the United States of America, the British Commonwealth, including Canada, and all other countries of the Copyright Union. All rights, including professional, amateur, motion picture, recitation, lecturing, public reading, radio broadcasting, television and the rights of translation into foreign languages are strictly reserved. In its present form the play is dedicated to the reading public only.

The amateur and professional live stage performance rights to *IT'S JUST SEX* are controlled exclusively by Samuel French, Inc., and licensing arrangements and performance licenses must be secured well in advance of presentation. PLEASE NOTE that amateur licensing fees are set upon application in accordance with your producing circumstances. When applying for a licensing quotation and a performance license please give us the number of performances intended, dates of production, your seating capacity and admission fee. Licensing fees are payable one week before the opening performance of the play to Samuel French, Inc., at 45 W. 25th Street, New York, NY 10010.

Licensing fee of the required amount must be paid whether the play is presented for charity or gain and whether or not admission is charged.

Professional/Stock licensing fees quoted upon application to Samuel French, Inc.

For all other rights than those stipulated above, apply to: Samuel French, Inc., at 45 W. 25th Street, New York, NY 10010.

Particular emphasis is laid on the question of amateur or professional readings, permission and terms for which must be secured in writing from Samuel French, Inc.

Copying from this book in whole or in part is strictly forbidden by law, and the right of performance is not transferable.

Whenever the play is produced the following notice must appear on all programs, printing and advertising for the play: "Produced by special arrangement with Samuel French, Inc."

Due authorship credit must be given on all programs, printing and advertising for the play.

ISBN 978-0-573-69938-2   Printed in U.S.A.   #29895

No one shall commit or authorize any act or omission by which the copyright of, or the right to copyright, this play may be impaired.

No one shall make any changes in this play for the purpose of production.

Publication of this play does not imply availability for performance. Both amateurs and professionals considering a production are strongly advised in their own interests to apply to Samuel French, Inc., for written permission before starting rehearsals, advertising, or booking a theatre.

No part of this book may be reproduced, stored in a retrieval system, or transmitted in any form, by any means, now known or yet to be invented, including mechanical, electronic, photocopying, recording, videotaping, or otherwise, without the prior written permission of the publisher.

MUSIC USE NOTE

Licensees are solely responsible for obtaining formal written permission from copyright owners to use copyrighted music in the performance of this play and are strongly cautioned to do so. If no such permission is obtained by the licensee, then the licensee must use only original music that the licensee owns and controls. Licensees are solely responsible and liable for all music clearances and shall indemnify the copyright owners of the play and their licensing agent, Samuel French, Inc., against any costs, expenses, losses and liabilities arising from the use of music by licensees.

IMPORTANT BILLING AND CREDIT REQUIREMENTS

All producers of *IT'S JUST SEX* must give credit to the Author of the Play in all programs distributed in connection with performances of the Play, and in all instances in which the title of the Play appears for the purposes of advertising, publicizing or otherwise exploiting the Play and/or a production. The name of the Author *must* appear on a separate line on which no other name appears, immediately following the title and *must* appear in size of type not less than fifty percent of the size of the title type.

IT'S JUST SEX was produced at the Two Roads Theater in Studio City, California, from Septemper 12, 2009 to November 6, 2010. The production was directed by Rick Shaw, produced by Rick Shaw and Shari Shaw, with the following cast:

JOAN	Rebecca Staub
PHIL	Scott Klace
CARL	Tommy Hinkley
KELLY	Jackie Debatin
GREG	Seth Peterson
LISA	Lisa Vidal
AMANDA	Meredith Giangrande, Erica Arana, India Summer

Succeeding cast:

JOAN	Mim Drew, Olivia d'Abo, Rachel Hollon, Jackie Debatin
PHIL	Michael Weaver, Blake Robbins, Alle Ghadban
CARL	Chris Payne Gilbert, Salvator Xuereb
KELLY	Kimberly Huie, Gina LaPiana
GREG	Gerald Downey, Caz Harleaux
LISA	Lisa Rotondi, Kalimba Bennett, Kristen Ariza, Georgia Hatzis

IT'S JUST SEX was initially presented at The Whitefire Theater in Sherman Oaks, California. The play was directed by Jeff Gould, with the following cast:

JOAN	Kristen Carey
PHIL	Steve Meadows
CARL	Bruce Nozick
KELLY	Summer Mahoney
GREG	Craig Woolson
LISA	Daintry Jensen
AMANDA	Amanda Swisten

IT'S JUST SEX was also produced at The Zephyr Theater, West Hollywood, California. There, it was directed by Jeff Gould, with the following cast:

JOAN	Carolyn Hennesy
PHIL	Eric Lutes
CARL	Thomas Calabro
KELLY	Janelle Giumarra
GREG	Bryan T. Donovan
LISA	Cate Cohen
AMANDA	Tiffany Ellen Solano

IT'S JUST SEX was presented at the Two Roads Theater, and was produced by Rick Shaw, directed by Mark Blanchard, and starred the following cast:

JOAN	Jamie Rose
PHIL	Matt Gerald
CARL	Orien Richman
KELLY	Betsy Russell
GREG	Sean Kanan
LISA	Sandra Purpuro
AMANDA	Natalia Fabia, Tammy Tomahawk

Also appearing as alternates were: Sharon Bristol-Kemp, Suzan Brittan, Scott Connell, Sean Douglas, Mark Durbin, Jeff Gould, Kelly Gullet. Jenifer Kingsley, Joanne Lubeck, Michelle O'Neill, Tracey Paleo, Greg Phelan, Forbes Riley, Donna Scott, Gillian Shure, Mark Sivertsen, Elisa Surmont. Special thanks to Shannon Monahan, Dan Hirsch, Patrick Baca, Joye Swan, and Dan Harrington.

CHARACTERS

JOAN - Personable, upscale housewife who can be bitingly sarcastic at times.

PHIL - Joan's husband. Well-groomed, charming, but serious, self-employed businessman.

GREG - Self-deprecating computer whiz that wishes he were more assertive, especially with his wife.

LISA - Greg's subtly controlling attorney wife. The work-hard/party-hard type.

CARL - Free spirited writer. He's horny and proud of it.

KELLY - Masseuse and Carl's wife. Pretty and sweet, yet clever at putting Carl in his place.

AMANDA - Sexy hooker.

A NOTE ON THE CASTING

There are six characters played by three men and three women. The seventh, and small role of Amanda, should ideally be played by a fourth actress, but if need be, can be doubled by Lisa or Kelly in disguise.

All characters are late thirties to early forties, except Amanda who is ideally early 20s, but could be older.

SETTING

The set is a contemporary upscale suburban living room. Stage right is a couch large enough to seat three, with a coffee table in front of it. Stage left is a bar with three bar stools around it. Upstage right, left, and center are doors or hallway openings, representing or leading to an unseen kitchen, the front door to the house, and three bedrooms. The room is nicely decorated. There is a flower vase and some type of CD music player on various shelves.

AUTHOR'S NOTE

I strongly advise keeping the pacing up throughout the entire play, especially in the second act. Obviously it is important not to rush key dramatic moments, and by all means, nail every comedic moment you can. But it can be easy, with this play, to fall into the trap of playing the second act too slow and too heavy.

ACT 1

Scene 1

(Lights up dimly on **PHIL** *– handsome, fortyish – and* **AMANDA** *– very sexy – standing up, grabbing, kissing, and playing around with each other.* **AMANDA** *is sexually toying with* **PHIL** *as he is as excited as can be.)*

AMANDA. *(stopping for a moment to look at each other)* You are so sexy.

PHIL. You're not so bad yourself.

*(***PHIL*** goes for her neck. Temperatures are rising.* **AMANDA** *suddenly pulls away from him.)*

What are you doing?

AMANDA. *(seductively)* Come and get me.

PHIL. I'm coming, baby! I'm coming!

(He starts chasing her around the room. After a few seconds, he catches up to her, and throws her down, on her back, on the couch. **AMANDA**'s *legs wind up spread wide, sticking up in the air like the letter "V".* **PHIL** *laughs and admires.)*

Wow, look at that. This is a Kodak moment!

(He grabs his cell phone and snaps a picture. Then he puts down the phone and flips her over.)

Turn over!

(He lifts her skirt, so that her rear end, which just has a skimpy thong on it, is exposed.)

AMANDA. Are we gonna get naughty now?

PHIL. *(enjoying)* I'm thinking about it. *(staring, at her proudly displayed rear end, with total admiration)* This is a work of art.

AMANDA. Glad you like it.

*(He feverishly starts kissing the cheeks of her rear end. At that moment the front door opens and **JOAN**, late thirties, nice looking, and well dressed, walks in. She sees them and looks shocked. **PHIL** and **AMANDA** don't hear her. **PHIL** continues kissing **AMANDA**'s rear end.)*

PHIL. This is delicious!

*(On that note, **JOAN** reaches for a switch and turns the lights on full. **PHIL** and **AMANDA** are startled and stop. For many seconds everyone in the room just takes in the situation without saying a word. Then **AMANDA** grabs her jacket and comes over to **PHIL** and puts her hand out wanting money. **PHIL**, mortified, quickly takes out some cash and hands it to her. **AMANDA** slowly counts it and even holds one of the bills up to the light to make sure it is good.)*

JOAN. *(watching it all)* Oh my God!

*(Finally **AMANDA** looks at **JOAN** and then **PHIL** and then...)*

AMANDA. ...I'll let myself out.

*(She walks right by **JOAN**. They exchange a glance. As **AMANDA** gets to the door, she turns back and motions the "call me" sign to **PHIL** and then exits.)*

PHIL. I'm sorry...I'm sorry.

*(**JOAN** walks off to the kitchen without saying a word.)*

What are you doing?

*(After a few moments, **JOAN** pops out of the kitchen with a smile, carrying a cleaning bucket. She is covering up and acting as if everything is wonderful, because she knows this will frustrate **PHIL**.)*

JOAN. Cleaning.

(She casually starts straightening things up.)

PHIL. Don't do this, Joan.

JOAN. I have to. Everybody's coming over tonight. Remember?

PHIL. *(remembering)* …Oh no.

JOAN. *(straightening the room)* My class was cancelled so I have plenty of time to make some food. I think everyone will be hungry, *(looking up at him with a smile)* although I can see you've already eaten.

PHIL. I forgot about tonight.

JOAN. That's understandable. You had a busy day.

*(On that note, **JOAN** liberally sprays air sanitizer all over the couch that **PHIL** and **AMANDA** were on. **PHIL** looks defeated.)*

PHIL. She's a hooker…that's all she is, just a hooker.

JOAN. Not everyone can be President.

PHIL. Are you gonna handle this just like everything else?

JOAN. What do you mean?

PHIL. Every time we have a problem, it's two seconds and Pfffft, right under the rug.

(He lifts the rug and points under it.)

Take a look. Here. Ten years of problems neatly swept away.

JOAN. Do we have a problem?

PHIL. *(looking up to the sky exasperated)* What can I do?

JOAN. You could cut up some vegetables.

PHIL. I'm gonna cancel tonight.

JOAN. No, you're not.

PHIL. We're not having company.

JOAN. Yes, we are.

PHIL. Is it image? Is that it? Is it always about our image?

JOAN. I'm not the one who needs a new car every year.

PHIL. It's for the business, Joan. In case you forgot, it's what pays for everything. So the kids can go to camp, so you can take yoga 36 times a week.

JOAN. *(finally having some reaction to what he says)* Fuck you, Phil.

PHIL. They're good friends. We're having a problem. They'll understand.

JOAN. *(back to being calm and in control)* We're having company.

PHIL. We have to talk.

JOAN. Start without me. I have to take a shower.

(She exits. **PHIL** *looks troubled. Lights down.)*

Scene 2

(There is a lighting change indicating that the same living room is now someone else's home. **CARL**, *late thirties and handsome is lounging on the couch.* **KELLY**, *very pretty, mid thirties enters from the bedroom.)*

KELLY. C'mon, we're supposed to be there at 7:30.

CARL. So what's the rush? It's only twenty-five after.

KELLY. Will you get your ass moving?

CARL. *(popping up)* I'd rather get your ass moving. Let's go fuck in public.

(He moves in on her.)

KELLY. Stop, I don't want to be late.

CARL. We won't. We'll be fashionably late. There's a difference.

KELLY. Oh, really?

CARL. Yes, it's acceptable. Everyone knows that fashionably late means you were screwing before you went out. That's why the term was invented.

*(**KELLY** looks at him like he's crazy.)*

KELLY. I'll be in the car.

(She starts for the door.)

CARL. Get-togethers are so boring. "How about that stock market. Seen any good movies lately?...Blah, blah, blah..."

KELLY. *(about to walk out)* Bye.

CARL. You're just anxious to see Phil.

KELLY. *(stopping in her tracks)* What?

CARL. I know you got a thing for him.

KELLY. I do not.

CARL. I've heard you talk about him a hundred times.

KELLY. Yeah, so, he's cute. That doesn't mean I want to sleep with him.

CARL. Yeah, but I think you do.

KELLY. I can control myself.

CARL. See that proves you want to sleep with him. Otherwise you'd have nothing to control.

(She looks at him sternly.)

I love it when you give me "The Look."

(He pulls her in and starts kissing her neck. She's stiff for a moment but softens quickly and starts to get into it.)

…See, you can't resist me.

KELLY. Shhh, I'm pretending you're Phil.

(CARL pulls back surprised, but not annoyed. With a pensive look, he contemplates what she said. After a moment, he smiles and…)

CARL. Whatever works.

(He goes for her again but she pushes him away.)

KELLY. Stop it.

(The chase is on. It is fun for both of them.)

CARL. C'mon baby.

KELLY. *(laughing)* Get away.

CARL. …Foreplay is so much fun.

KELLY. Stop.

(She makes a quick move and runs out the door.)

CARL. *(going after her)* C'mon baby, come to Phil!

(He exits.)

Scene 3

(There is a lighting change indicating yet another home.)

*(**GREG**, late thirties, sitting on the couch looking dejected. **LISA**, mid to late thirties comes out and sees him.)*

LISA. It's no big deal.

GREG. That's what you said the last time.

LISA. It happens to all men.

GREG. *(sarcastic)* Thanks, I feel much better now.

LISA. *(like rapid fire and in complete control)* Here's what you need to do. Relax, have a drink, call Phil and Joan and cancel tonight, take out a porno and we'll try again.

GREG. *(sarcastic)* Wait, I need a pen. I didn't get all of that.

LISA. You're putting too much pressure on yourself.

GREG. *(slightly accusing)* Oh, is that what the problem is?

LISA. What does that mean?

GREG. Nothing.

LISA. Let me guess. It's my fault. You hate it when I'm aggressive. It turns you off.

GREG. No, it doesn't. And don't do that.

LISA. Do what?

GREG. The "it's all my fault" routine. It's not your fault.

LISA. Ok, and it's not your fault either.

GREG. Ok, so it's nobody's fault.

LISA. Fine.

GREG. *(getting the last word in)* Fine!

LISA. *(after a few beats)* …If you'd just watch those DVD's I bought you.

GREG. You just have to keep it up, don't you?

LISA. *(She can't resist)* Well, somebody has to.

GREG. *(fake laugh)* The jokes really help. My penis is hitting the ceiling.

(She laughs.)

C'mon, let's go. We're going to be late.

LISA. *(sudden idea)* Let's cancel tonight.
GREG. What?
LISA. Let's go dancing!
GREG. Dancing?

(She starts dancing and shaking her hips around him, while he stands there like a stick in the mud.)

LISA. Yeah, it'll be great. Call Phil and Joan and tell 'em we're sick.
GREG. I can't.
LISA. *(still dancing)* Why not?
GREG. What if somebody sees us?
LISA. Who's gonna see us there?
GREG. I don't know, somebody…I just know if we lie about it, something'll happen. I'll fall down, break my leg, get rushed away in an ambulance, the ambulance will drive through their neighborhood and get a flat tire right in front of their house. It never fails.
LISA. *(sarcastic)* …I didn't think of that.
GREG. Besides, I thought you like these get-togethers.
LISA. I do, I just want something more tonight.
GREG. I know! You wanna hold-up a few gas stations?
LISA. *(playing along and wishing he means it)* Ok!
GREG. *(letting her down)* Great. You get the gun. I'll start the car.

*(On that note, **GREG** goes out leaving her alone. **LISA** sighs and follows.)*

Scene 4

(Another lighting change and we're back to **PHIL** *and* **JOAN***'s place.* **JOAN** *is standing at the bar, drinking from a large glass of scotch.* **PHIL** *comes out from the bedroom and exchanges an uncomfortable glance with* **JOAN**. **JOAN** *tidies something up while* **PHIL** *watches. The doorbell rings.* **PHIL** *makes a move for the door, but* **JOAN** *motions that she will answer it.* **PHIL** *accommodates.* **JOAN** *walks to the door looking serious. She gets there, takes a deep breath, and completely and instantly changes her demeanor for the guests. She opens the door with a huge smile, vivacious as ever.)*

JOAN. Hi!!!

*(***CARL** *and* **KELLY** *enter.)*

CARL/KELLY. Hi.

JOAN. Come on in.

(She hugs them both.)

PHIL. Carl, Kelly.

KELLY. Phil!

*(***KELLY** *comes across the room to* **PHIL** *and gives him a warm embrace.* **CARL** *stands center stage watching, and nods his head with a devilish smile as* **KELLY** *hugs* **PHIL**.*)*

PHIL. *(finally breaking the hug)* ...Anybody thirsty?

*(***CARL** *raises his hand)*

KELLY. I thought you'd never ask.

PHIL. *(To* **KELLY**, *as he moves toward the bar)* All right, let's see, vodka and cranberry?

(To **CARL***)* And, a screwdriver?

CARL. The man is good.

KELLY. That he is.

*(Winks at **CARL** as she refers to **PHIL**. **CARL** is not jealous, but nevertheless, gestures with his fingers to his eyes, as if to say, "I'm watching you.")*

CARL. So, where's Greg and Lisa?

JOAN. Fashionably late I guess.

CARL. Oh, at least somebody is.

*(**CARL** clears his throat and elbows **KELLY** on that one.)*

JOAN. ...So, Carl, any new books on the way?

CARL. Nah, been looking for something interesting to write about.

JOAN. You ought to talk to Phil. He's always has something interesting going on.

PHIL. *(trying to get past Joan's crack)* ...So how about that stock market?

CARL. *(feigning interest)* Oh yeah, it's really something.

*(The doorbell rings. **JOAN** answers it.)*

JOAN. Greg, Lisa. The party's just heating up. Come on in.

GREG. *(bolting right in)* I have a question for everyone. From our house to your house, is it quicker to take the streets or the freeway?*

LISA. Nobody cares, Greg.

GREG. You did when I was driving here. *(back to the others:)* So what do you think, streets or freeway?

JOAN. Streets.

GREG. What?!

PHIL. I agree, streets.

*(**LISA** looks triumphant.)*

GREG. How can you say that? There are no lights on the freeway.

PHIL. Yeah, but it's only one exit and you gotta go out of the way to get to it.

GREG. You're all nuts.

---

* Freeway can be changed to expressway, parkway, or whatever fits the region

KELLY. Why don't you do a computer analysis of it?

GREG. I bet if I take the freeway, I could beat someone taking the streets.

CARL. Watch it, Lisa. Your husband's about to gamble away the family fortune.

GREG. You think I'm wrong too?

CARL. *(laughs)* I haven't the vaguest idea, nor do I give a shit.

LISA. It's ok, honey. You're not always wrong, just most of the time.

PHIL. …All right, let's see, Greg wants a light beer.

GREG. No, tequila.

PHIL. Ooh! Ok. And Lisa will have a gin and tonic?

LISA. Ok…Uh, you know what? Why don't you hold the tonic tonight.

JOAN. You go girl.

PHIL. Coming up.

GREG. *(obsessing)* I know I could do it quicker on the freeway.

LISA. Well, why don't you spend the night driving it a bunch of times, while we stay here and party.

CARL. *(checking his watch)* Yeah, I'll time you if you want. On your mark, get set, go.

GREG. On your mark, get set, bite me.

KELLY. …So what did everybody do today?

*(**PHIL**, **JOAN**, **GREG** and **LISA** all just stand there speechless. There is a long awkward pause. **KELLY** and **CARL** look a little puzzled.)*

…Ok, what's everybody doing tomorrow?

(Everyone responds immediately to that one.)

JOAN. Tennis.

PHIL. Work.

GREG/LISA. Dancing.

CARL. Much better question, honey.

LISA. Let's play a game.

CARL. Huh?

LISA. I've decided we should play a game tonight.

CARL. What kind of game?

GREG. *(interrupts)* Here she goes.

LISA. What?

GREG. *(to the others)* Ever since the kids left for camp she's been on this mission for us to have a good time. She's been planning out every single second.

LISA. So…?

GREG. *(to LISA)* So, it's too much. Just once in our lives it would be nice to do something and have no idea what's gonna happen.

LISA. *(taps GREG on the knee)* We already had that tonight, Honey.

(GREG scowls. The others are clueless.)

KELLY. Joan, I haven't seen you since the school fair. You look great.

JOAN. Thanks, I've been taking yoga like 36 times a week.

(She pointedly yells the "36 times" part in PHIL's direction referring to his earlier yoga comment.)

LISA. *(crossing to stand next to the other women, while the men are bunched around the bar)* Speaking of the fair, did you see Marcy Cohen's boob job?

JOAN. I know. Think they're big enough?

LISA. Echh! Gross.

CARL. *(sarcastically)* Yeah, horrendous.

(All three men raise and clink glasses.)

KELLY. Anybody miss the kids yet?

CARL. Yeah, I really miss the whining.

PHIL. Don't forget the chauffeuring.

LISA. I can't live without the fighting.

JOAN. I miss the mess.

GREG. No, no, the constant racket.

LISA. It's the weirdest thing. I went to work every day this week, and I feel like I'm on vacation.

(They all laugh.)

JOAN. How about a toast. To freedom! Two whole months of it.

*(They all take a drink. After **CARL** finishes his sip he moves toward **KELLY** and playfully goes for her neck. She gently avoids it.)*

KELLY. Easy tiger.

CARL. I can't help it. I crave you.

KELLY. You crave anybody.

CARL. *(pauses and looks at her for a moment)* …Yeah, but you're one of them.

KELLY. *(playfully to the others)* I actually married him, didn't I?

JOAN. I'm afraid so, Kel.

LISA. Sorry, better luck next time.

CARL. Listen to you guys. See, that's the problem with marriage. Women have it so good and they don't even know it.

KELLY. Oh, really?

CARL. Yeah, marriage is totally designed for you. We're not hard wired for monogamy. So when we get married, we have to give something up and you don't.

KELLY. Why do men always act like it's the ultimate sacrifice not to screw one hundred different women?

CARL/GREG/PHIL. *(serious, like it's obvious)* …Because it is.

KELLY. Poor babies.

CARL. How would you like it if you weren't allowed to talk?

KELLY. What!!??

CARL. I mean it. How would you like it, if any time you had the urge to say something, you had to stifle it or society would call you slime.

KELLY. I'm getting the urge to say something right now.

CARL. No, I think I hit the nail on the head here. A woman's desire to talk is the same as a man's desire to have sex.

(On that note, he turns toward PHIL for a "High 5", but PHIL, who wants nothing to do with this conversation, just shakes his head and looks down, trying to avoid CARL.)

KELLY. Honey, you're allowed to have sex. Only with me.

CARL. What if I was the only one you could talk to?

KELLY. *(with a sour look)* ...Oooh.

LISA. Sometimes it scares me when he makes sense.

GREG. I still think the freeway's quicker.

JOAN. Have another drink, Greg?

PHIL. How's work going, buddy?

GREG. I don't know. I guess it's been getting to me a little lately.

PHIL. I thought you loved computers?

GREG. I do, but I don't know. After 12 years you can get bored of anything. I'd probably get tired of being a porn star if I did it long enough.

(GREG laughs as he says this. As GREG is laughing, LISA slowly turns her head toward him as if about to comment on the thought of him being a porn star. As he sees LISA, GREG's facial expression suddenly changes and he authoritatively says...)

Don't.

(LISA puts her hand over her mouth and stifles herself.)

...I just feel like I'm stuck in a rut.

(There is a quiet moment as they all relate to GREG's comment.)

JOAN. ...Hey, Lisa's right. Let's play a game.

PHIL. Huh?

JOAN. I think it's a great idea.

LISA. Yeah, let's do it.

PHIL. What kind of game?

CARL. How about spin the bottle?

LISA. *(laughs)* We used to play that at sixth grade parties.

PHIL. Another five minutes, the scotch bottle should be empty.

JOAN. Let's play a drinking game.

PHIL. Make that two minutes.

LISA. We did that at high school parties.

JOAN. Good, so we'll regress a little. C'mon let's do it.

GREG. I think she's serious.

CARL. I'm hungry. Could we make it an eating game?

JOAN. Does that mean you're in?

CARL. What do you think?

JOAN. Good. How about you Kelly? Carl likes the idea.

KELLY. Are you trying to convince me or talk me out of it?

JOAN. I'll take that as a yes…Greg?

GREG. Can I get drunk first and think about it?

JOAN. All right. We're all set.

KELLY. We haven't heard from Phil yet.

JOAN. *(with absolutely no regard for Phil's wishes)* He'll play.

(PHIL squirms.)

So, does everybody have a drink?

(They all acknowledge.)

Let's do it.

LISA. Are we gonna play a word game?

JOAN. No, I have a better idea. Let's play "Tell the Truth."

(A round of "Huhs?" are heard throughout the room.)

CARL. That's a game?

GREG. Isn't that a TV show?

JOAN. Everybody has to reveal something that the rest of us don't know. If we…

CARL. *(interrupting)* No, no I hate these games!

JOAN. *(continuing right over him)* If we think it's bullshit or no big deal, you have to drink. If it's a good one, everybody else drinks.

PHIL. I think that's been done before.

JOAN. *(right back to him)* Good, then I guess your day will be full of things that have been done before.

LISA. What if we can't think of anything?

JOAN. You will. Everybody has secrets. All right, when it's your turn you have to come up with something. Now who's gonna start us off?…How about Carl?

CARL. Why me?

JOAN. You're a free-spirit. This game's right up your alley.

LISA. Yeah, c'mon Carl. You can come up with something.

CARL. …All right. I'll give it a shot.

JOAN. There we go.

CARL. You ready…I used to be a woman.

(Everybody laughs and mutters to themselves.)

JOAN. C'mon Carl, be serious.

PHIL. I believe him!

LISA. Is it true, Kelly?

KELLY. I don't even think he's human.

JOAN. Bad one Carl, drink up.

CARL. What? C'mon, I can't reveal anything bigger than that.

JOAN. Drink.

(He drinks.)

We'll come back to you. Lisa, you're up.

LISA. Oh, ok, I have one. I'm an honest lawyer.

(Everyone takes it in for a beat and then, almost robotically, they all drink at the same time and playfully share a laugh about it.)

CARL. Nobody's gonna top that one.

JOAN. We'll let you get away with that one for now. How about you, Kelly?

KELLY. Uh oh.

CARL. C'mon Kel, give us a juicy one.

KELLY. Do I have to?

CARL. Yeah, c'mon. You wanna get us thrown out of the party?

KELLY. ...All right...I have one. A guy came on to me during a massage last week.

(A few oohs and aahs around the room.)

CARL. *(Not bothered at all)* Just one guy?

GREG. What happened?

KELLY. It was no big deal. He just kind of started rubbing my leg a little. At first I tried to ignore it, but then he grabbed my ass.

JOAN. Did you throw him out?

KELLY. No, I just told him that was against the rules and he stopped.

JOAN. Men are something.

CARL. *(proudly)* That, we are.

GREG. *(To CARL)* That doesn't bother you?

CARL. *(To KELLY)* Did he hurt you?

KELLY. No.

CARL. *(Back to GREG)* It doesn't bother me.

JOAN. Good job, Kelly. Drink up everyone.

(They all drink.)

Ok, Greg, you're turn.

GREG. No Joan, I'm boring.

JOAN. Yes, you are boring, but you still have to take a turn.

GREG. Oh boy...Uhh...All right, I got one. To get my job...I lied on my resume.

CARL. *(mocking him)* Ooooooh! You animal!

GREG. You don't understand. I made up practically everything.

CARL. That's what resumes are for. They're a bullshitting contest. Best bullshitter gets the job.

GREG. *(To JOAN)* What's the ruling?

JOAN. An honest attempt. We all drink.

(A bunch of objections are heard around the room.)

An honest attempt. We all drink.

KELLY. How about you Joan? What don't we know about your life?

JOAN. Couple of things.

PHIL. *(interrupting, afraid of what JOAN might say)* Can I take a turn?

JOAN. Sure Phil. Go ahead.

PHIL. All right…um…Now I forgot what I was going to say.

JOAN. C'mon Phil. You must have something.

PHIL. *(trying to get out of it)* …I wet the bed till I was nine years old.

GREG. Oh, don't start with the childhood stuff.

LISA. That's a pretty good one.

CARL. Big deal. I'm over forty and I still do it.

KELLY. Those are wet dreams, honey.

CARL. Oh.

KELLY. Now it's Joan's turn.

JOAN. Ok, I have one.

PHIL. *(afraid of what she might say)* Joan, don't.

CARL. Hey, you had your pee pee story. Let her go.

(PHIL nervously backs off.)

JOAN. I didn't lose my virginity until I was 23.

CARL. *(as if it truly is sad)* Oh, how sad.

LISA. Weren't you already with Phil then?

JOAN. Uh huh.

CARL. Ooh! Now, it's a tragedy.

PHIL. Very funny.

GREG. Why'd you wait so long?

JOAN. Everyone makes mistakes.

(An uncomfortable silence follows.)

CARL. …I need to reload.

JOAN. Ok, refills for everyone.

PHIL. I got it.

(They all start to get drinks.)

JOAN. Ok, let's get ready for round two.

KELLY. We have to go again?

JOAN. Yeah, everybody's not drunk yet.

KELLY. I'm getting there.

JOAN. Good, let's keep going. All right let's kick this game into second gear. Who's got a big one to start us off?

CARL. *(grabs his crotch)* I have one.

KELLY. Behave.

JOAN. Anybody?

GREG. I have one

(Everyone looks at him. He holds for a few seconds.)

…nevermind.

JOAN. What is it Greg?

GREG. Nothing, Somebody else go.

CARL. I want to hear this one.

KELLY. It's ok, Greg. Whatever it is.

*(**GREG** just looks at them.)*

GREG. Forget it.

(He looks troubled.)

JOAN. Just get it over with.

GREG. It might ruin the party.

JOAN. Nonsense. Just tell us.

GREG. *(Again he looks around at everyone. Then he takes a deep breath and…)* …I have six months to live.

*(A silence comes over the room. Everyone just looks at him while he looks back at them with a somber face. **LISA** looks completely stunned. Finally, after a few moments…)*

Bam!! Got ya!

(**GREG** *does a little celebration dance as he is so proud of his joke.*)

KELLY. Oh you little bullshit artist.

CARL. I almost bought it for a second.

LISA. That's the stupidest joke I've ever heard.

PHIL. I want to see that resume.

JOAN. *(admiringly)* I didn't know you had it in you.

GREG. *(loving it)* Drink up, bitches.

LISA. No you drink.

JOAN. Let's all drink on that one.

(They do.)

All right, Lisa.

LISA. …Ok…I'm bored with my life.

GREG. *(sarcastic)* Thanks, honey.

LISA. It's not you, it's… I have everything I ever dreamed of. I'm a successful lawyer. I have a wonderful husband, two beautiful children, a nice house, and I'm bored. Why is that?

CARL. Cause there's nothing good on TV.

KELLY. Sounds like a mid-life crisis.

CARL. See, that's the kind of shit on TV, reality shows and mid-life crises.

PHIL. Yeah, and what are you writing about?

CARL. Sex. That's what everybody's interested in.

KELLY. Every man.

CARL. And every woman. Some of them just don't know it or won't admit it.

KELLY. Thank you for enlightening us, honey.

CARL. My pleasure.

KELLY. I still think it's a mid-life crisis. I hear it every day at work.

JOAN. What do you hear?

KELLY. Oh…"I should have done this with my life"…"I never should have done that"…You know.

LISA. I don't have a lot of regrets. I'm just…restless.

GREG. Well, why don't you get a massage from Kelly, put your hand on her ass and tell her all about it. Meanwhile, whose turn is it?

JOAN. Hold it. We didn't drink yet.

(holds up her glass)

To no more boredom.

(They all drink.)

All right Carl, how about a real one this time?

(JOAN goes behind the couch where CARL is sitting.)

CARL. You need me to liven up your party, huh?

JOAN. That's why I invited you.

CARL. Something real, huh?

JOAN. No bullshit this time.

LISA. *(comes over and sits on the arm of the couch next to CARL)* Yeah, c'mon Carl. Give us something juicy.

CARL. *(with all three women around him)* All right…I fantasized about us all swapping tonight.

(They all start laughing at CARL being CARL.)

PHIL. …That sounds like Carl.

GREG. *(humoring)* Who do you want, my wife or his?

CARL. My mind's open.

PHIL. Open isn't the word I'd use to describe your mind.

JOAN. *(humoring)* What do you think, Kelly?

KELLY. I'd probably do it, but who'd want Carl.

CARL. *(looking at LISA)* You wanted something juicy, Lisa.

LISA. I didn't say anything.

GREG. …What does that mean?

LISA. What does what mean?

GREG. What kind of reaction is that?

LISA. I don't know. It's a nothing reaction.

GREG. You like the idea.

LISA. I didn't say a word. Joan, whose turn is it?

JOAN. I think it's still Carl's turn.

CARL. What? That wasn't enough? Do I have to do the pairing too?

PHIL. You're a sick man.

JOAN. But an honest man. I'll drink to that.

PHIL. Wait a second. I want something real out of Carl. Everyone else is revealing stuff and all you do is make jokes.

CARL. I never joke about sex.

PHIL. C'mon Carl, tell us something we don't already know.

CARL. Like what? What do you want to hear? I can't swim, I'm afraid of the dark, I once pooped in my pants… Nobody cares about any of that.

GREG. You pooped in your pants?

CARL. It figures you'd focus on that.

KELLY. Let's play something else.

GREG. *(joking around)* All right. How about a little strip poker?

KELLY. That's not what I had in mind.

GREG. Are you kidding? It's perfect. That's how we'll pair off. Whichever two people are naked first have sex.

(They all chuckle.)

CARL. *(after the chuckling dies down)* …What if it's you and me?

GREG. *(playing back at him)* …I'm on top.

KELLY. What about Charades or Trivial Pursuit?

PHIL. Why do we have to play a game? How about just talking?

CARL. We can't. We did that last time.

LISA. Last two times, I think.

CARL. She's right. *(To **PHIL**)* It's gotta be a game.

KELLY. I know! How about Monopoly?

(Everyone looks at her like she's crazy.)

…Nevermind.

JOAN. Let's keep playing this game. We're learning things. That's what life's all about. It's amazing how many things we don't know about people. Ok, Phil, you're up. Why don't you tell us another peepee story?

PHIL. I'll pass.

JOAN. You can't pass. We're playing a game.

PHIL. Come back to me.

JOAN. C'mon, there must be some other secret you want to share with the group.

PHIL. Cut it out, Joan.

JOAN. All right, nevermind. We'll skip your turn. It's CHEATING! But so what. Ok, Lisa, what do you got?

LISA. I guess I have one.

JOAN. Let's hear it.

LISA. …maybe I shouldn't.

JOAN. Too late, you already started. What is it?

LISA. …I once did it with two guys at the same time.

JOAN. Really?

CARL. Congratulations.

GREG. *(gradually perking up and looking puzzled)* …You never told me that.

LISA. It was only one time.

GREG. When?

LISA. Last week.

*(**GREG**'s eyes bulge out of his head. **LISA** looks serious and holds the moment for a few seconds.)*

…Bam!! Got ya!

*(She dances and celebrates just as **GREG** did with his six months to live comment from before)*

I'm just kidding. It was back in college, one night when I got really drunk.

CARL. How was it?

LISA. It wasn't boring.

GREG. *(whining)* I never did that.

CARL. You've never been with two guys?

GREG. *(sarcastically)* Not at the same time.

(*To* **LISA**)

How come you never told me about that?

LISA. It's not the kind of thing that comes up all the time.

(**GREG** *is a little stunned.*)

JOAN. Good job, Lisa. Drink time everyone.

(*They all drink.*)

Greg, if you want to jump in again you can. Your wife just gave us a juicy one.

(*lost in thought*)

…Greg, are you with us?

GREG. …Huh, yeah, what?

JOAN. What are you thinking about?

GREG. *(dejectedly)* My college days. I wasted them on an education.

(*They all laugh.*)

JOAN. All right, Kelly, you must have some juicy ones.

KELLY. None that I want to talk about.

JOAN. Oh, so you have a few stories too?

KELLY. I guess I've had my moments.

CARL. Well, c'mon, lay one on us.

KELLY. Maybe after another ten or twenty drinks.

CARL. Boo! That's a cop out. I think she has to drink for that. What do you say, Joan?

JOAN. Absolutely.

KELLY. *(takes the easy way out)* I'd be happy to.

(*She drinks.*)

JOAN. You're not getting off that easy. We'll come back to you.

KELLY. I'll be here.

JOAN. All right, I guess we're back to me.

CARL. Yeah, c'mon, Joan. Show us how this game is really supposed to be played.

JOAN. Ok, I have one…I think swapping's a good idea.

(Everyone just looks at her. **CARL** *looks triumphant.)*

PHIL. What are you doing?

JOAN. Just telling the truth. What do you say everyone? Should we do it?

PHIL. Stop it, Joan.

JOAN. Stop what? Life is short. Let's live a little.

(No one responds)

…C'mon everyone. Don't tell me it's never crossed your minds. Because I know it has.

PHIL. *(trying to remain calm)* Ok, dear, that's enough.

JOAN. Enough? We're just getting started. C'mon, everyone. We've been getting together for years. There isn't one person in this room who can look me in the eye and tell me they never thought about sleeping with someone else. Is there?

KELLY. Even if the thought has crossed our minds, people think about murder, but that doesn't mean they're gonna run out and do it.

JOAN. So you have thought about it. Thank you, Kelly.

KELLY. That's not what I was trying to…

JOAN. *(cutting her off)* What about you Lisa? You're bored with life. Haven't you ever thought about it?

LISA. *(no hesitation)* Yep.

GREG. …That was an easy one.

LISA. I'm just being honest.

GREG. Who do you want?

LISA. I don't want anyone. I'm just admitting the thought has crossed my mind.

GREG. How often?

LISA. Greg…

(He backs off.)

JOAN. Good for you, Lisa.

KELLY. Maybe we should talk about something else.

CARL. Honey, it's rude to interrupt.

(**KELLY** *just gives him a look.*)

JOAN. No, let's talk about this. Talk is good. Never sweep anything under the rug.

PHIL. *(trying to calmly diffuse the whole thing)* I think you're disturbing our guests, dear.

JOAN. I don't think so, but let's ask them. Am I disturbing anyone?

(Nobody answers.)

…I didn't think so. So what about you, Kelly? I'll bet you're as open to this as anyone in the room.

KELLY. Why do you say that?

JOAN. First of all, you're married to Carl, so you must have an open mind. And secondly, I've seen the way you look at my husband.

KELLY. *(embarrassed)* I do not.

JOAN. Yes, you do. Ask anyone in the room.

(Everyone puts their heads down simultaneously, not wanting to respond.)

KELLY. …I'll admit that I think Phil is a good looking man, but that doesn't mean anything. Greg and, uh, uh… *(She pauses for a moment as she momentarily stumbles)*… Carl are good looking, too.

CARL. *(shocked, but never angry)* You forgot my name! I can't believe you forgot my name.

(Everyone laughs.)

PHIL. I don't believe this discussion. *(To* **JOAN***)* Look what you're doing to Kelly.

KELLY. It's ok, Phil. I'm all right.

JOAN. See Phil, everyone's all right, but you.

CARL. Yeah, we're just keeping the conversation lively, that's all.

JOAN. Now let's see...I have to admit that I find both Greg and Carl attractive. They're both appealing in a different sort of way. Don't you agree, Lisa?

LISA. *(staying neutral)* All the men in this room are very attractive, Joan.

CARL. Such a lawyer.

JOAN. So Carl, what do you think?

CARL. I think that Phil and Greg are both very attractive.

JOAN. Tell us about your fantasy. Who were you with?

CARL. *(referring to all three women)* Oh, I was pretty much here, there, and everywhere.

JOAN. I can believe that. How about you, Greg? You know, it's never too late to make up for lost time.

(GREG ponders it all.)

GREG. Maybe you're right.

PHIL. Anybody want to get back to the game? I'll take a turn.

JOAN. The game's over, Phil. We're moving on to another game now.

PHIL. You know sometimes you can take a joke too far.

JOAN. I'm not joking. Is anybody joking?

PHIL. I know my wife has had a little too much to drink, but where's everyone else at?

CARL. We're just talking.

LISA. Yeah, it's no big deal. We're just talking.

PHIL. Well, just in case the talk keeps going, I'd like to point out that we all have lives, marriages and families that could be affected by this kind of talk.

JOAN. *(mocking)* Ooh, careful everyone. Our lives may be in danger!

KELLY. Maybe he's right, Joan.

JOAN. Oh, c'mon Kelly, not you too. Tonight is special. We're putting all the bullshit away. Now Kelly, tell us honestly. What are you really thinking?

KELLY. I'll admit that once in a while I have certain desires, but sometimes you have to think about the consequences.

JOAN. Everything you do in life has consequences, but you can't stop living. Sometimes you just gotta have fun and do what you want.

PHIL. And sometimes you can't.

JOAN. Yes, I guess the key is knowing which is which.

PHIL. I guess it is.

JOAN. Too many people are stifling their impulses. It's no way to go through life. You can never have any fun that way. Sometimes you just gotta do what you want, when you want.

(She guzzles her drink and then offers out her hand.)

Greg...

(Everyone laughs, not taking her seriously.)

*(**JOAN** walks over to **GREG** and takes him by the hand. **GREG** laughs and playfully goes along with it. They move toward the bedroom.)*

LISA. *(laughing)* Good luck, Joan.

*(**GREG** does a quick double take at **LISA**'s dig. Just as they get near the bedroom **GREG** lets go of **JOAN**'s hand, as if the joke is finally over. However, **JOAN** pulls him back to her and gives him a big kiss right in front of **PHIL**. A moment later, looking dead serious, she leads him away. **GREG** looks like a deer in headlights as he is pulled off stage into a bedroom. **JOAN** shoots a final look at **PHIL** as if to say, "Take that, asshole!," and then she exits. The others all look surprised, except **CARL** who looks quite pleased by the developments. **PHIL** is shocked. He doesn't know what to do. After a long beat, **KELLY** studies her husband, takes another gulp of her drink, and then walks over to **PHIL** and puts out her hand just like **JOAN** did to **GREG**.)*

PHIL. No, Kelly, I can't do that.

KELLY. It's ok, Phil. Carl doesn't care.

(**KELLY** *slowly starts leading* **PHIL** *off. He reluctantly moves with her. Just as he is about to go off with* **KELLY**, **PHIL** *looks at* **CARL** *as if to ask, "Are you ok with this?"* **CARL** *immediately gives him the "Thumbs up" sign, and* **KELLY** *drags* **PHIL** *off to a second bedroom.* **CARL** *and* **LISA** *are now the only ones left.* **CARL** *is beaming.*)

CARL. *(Shrugs his shoulders)* …Monopoly?

(**LISA** *laughs.*)

LISA. …How many bedrooms do they have in this house?

(**CARL** *gets up and puts his hand out for* **LISA**. *She gets up, they join hands, and walk off to a third bedroom. Lights out.*)

(*The stage is now momentarily dark. The actors are backstage behind the rear walls. These walls are special material, that when spotlighted from behind, show each couple in silhouette. One at a time, spotlights highlight the three areas. When each couple is spotlighted, they can be seen in silhouette acting out the following brief scenes, while the other two couples are dark. As we switch from room to room, an appropriate song for that couple is heard.*)

(*From one room:*)

GREG. You redecorated.

JOAN. *(pushing* **GREG** *around)* Take your pants off!

GREG. *(looking down)* Hey, a Persian rug.

JOAN. *(turning him)* Shut up, Greg!

GREG. *(looking up)* …Oh, and a skylight too.

JOAN. *(totally taking charge)* Kiss me, Greg.

(*Switch to another room:*)

PHIL. *(ecstatic moan)* Oh, that feels good.

KELLY. *(rubbing* **PHIL**'s *shoulders)* Phil, you're carrying so much tension.

PHIL. Yeah, I've had a busy day.

(From the third room:)

LISA. *(They are having vigorous sex. They are both standing with LISA bent over and CARL behind her.)* Oh yeah! oh yeah!

CARL. Yeah, baby! Yeah baby!

LISA. *(Building)* Oh Greg! Oh Greg!

CARL. ...I'm Carl!

(back to room one:)

JOAN. *(They are in each other's arms.)* Greg, that was incredible.

GREG. Yeah?

JOAN. Let's do it again.

GREG. Really?

JOAN. I want to give you something real to put on that resume.

(room two:)

PHIL. *(They are caressing each other.)* Kelly, isn't this better than Monopoly?

KELLY. Phil, isn't it weird being with another woman in your own home?

PHIL. ...Not really.

(third room:)

LISA. *(still going at it)* Oh yeah, Oh yeah!

CARL. Yeah, baby! Yeah, baby!

LISA. Oh God!! Oh God!!

CARL. ...I told you, I'm Carl.

END OF ACT ONE

(Ideally, the play should now continue on to Act II, without breaking for intermission.)

ACT 2

Scene 1

(The same living room a half hour later. No one is onstage. After a moment **CARL** *and* **LISA** *enter from the bedroom. They both look around to see if anyone else is there. They exchange a slightly uncomfortable smile.)*

CARL. …I guess we're first.

LISA. I guess so.

CARL. …How embarrassing for me…You want a drink?

LISA. Oh yeah.

*(***LISA*** sits on the couch.* **CARL** *goes to the bar to get some drinks.)*

CARL. …We ought to have game night more often.

*(***CARL*** brings the drinks over. He spots potato chips from before. He starts eating.)*

I can't believe how hungry I am.

LISA. …How long do we wait?

CARL. As long as it takes.

LISA. …So…Seen any good movies lately?

*(***CARL*** laughs at her question.)*

…What…

CARL. Nothing, it's just that earlier, Kelly and I were talking about party conversations…

(Just then **PHIL** *and* **KELLY** *enter from the bedroom and see* **CARL** *and* **LISA** *on the couch. Everyone studies each other for a moment. The air is uneasy.* **KELLY** *walks by* **LISA***, giving her a dirty look and then she goes to the*

bar. Meanwhile **PHIL** *starts pacing around the room. He tries to listen where* **JOAN** *and* **GREG** *went off. He eventually works his way over to* **CARL**, *who is now voraciously eating chips.* **PHIL** *just watches in disbelief at* **CARL**'s *obsession with eating.)*

PHIL. *(finally after several seconds of watching* **CARL** *stuff his face)* …Good?

*(***CARL***hesitates for a moment as he's not sure what* **PHIL** *is referring to. He looks at* **LISA**, *then the chips, then* **LISA** *again, then back to* **PHIL**.*)*

CARL. …The chips?

PHIL. *(like it was obvious)* The chips.

CARL. *(nodding)* …Good.

(After a few moments of silence **PHIL**, *looking troubled, starts pacing right in front of them.)*

KELLY. *(to* **CARL***)* I think we should leave.

CARL. *(off* **PHIL***'s pacing around)* I ain't missing this!

*(***PHIL** *continues to pace as the others watch.)*

LISA. …I'm sure they'll be out soon.

PHIL. *(like it's no big deal)* Whenever.

KELLY. …So how's business, Phil?

PHIL. Fine.

KELLY. That's good…Does anyone want to talk about this?

(The others all give her a disapproving look, except **CARL**, *who raises his hand.* **KELLY** *just turns away.)*

…Forget it.

(A few more moments of uncomfortable tension go by)

CARL. …So how about that stock market?

LISA. I know, it's really something.

CARL. Up and down, and up and down, and up and down…

*(***CARL***'s delivery and gestures are sexually suggestive, which further remind* **PHIL** *of what is going on with his wife and* **GREG**.*)*

PHIL. *(suddenly)* That's enough!!

(He quickly moves toward the bedroom.)

CARL. *(jumping up to get in his way)* Phil, I don't think you should!

PHIL. *(very agitated)* I don't give a shit what you think right now!

LISA. Don't, Phil!

*(**PHIL** is more receptive to **LISA** and stops. He also looks at **KELLY** who shakes her head in disapproval. He comes back in to the room.)*

CARL. Why don't you try to relax, Phil.

PHIL. I'm fine, Carl.

CARL. Can I offer you anything?

*(As he says this, he playfully gestures to **KELLY**, as if he is offering up his wife again. **KELLY** shoves him away like he's a nut, but **CARL** just laughs.)*

*(After a few seconds **GREG** slowly enters from the bedroom. He looks completely disheveled. His shirt is hanging out of his pants, his hair is completely messed up, he's carrying one of his shoes in his hand, and the overwhelmed expression on his face is as if he just came off the roller coaster ride of his life. **JOAN** is right behind him, with a devilish smile, looking cocky as can be. **GREG** uncomfortably walks by **PHIL** and sits down next to **LISA**. The air is uneasy.)*

GREG. *(To **LISA**)* I think we should be going.

PHIL. *(acting a little strange)* Relax. It's early. Have a seat. Anybody need a drink? Anybody…anything?

(No one responds.)

*(He comes and sits on the arm of the couch near **GREG**)*

So Greg, did you have fun with my wife?

*(**GREG** is speechless.)*

Greg…are you Ok?

JOAN. He's probably too worn out to talk.

(**PHIL** *tries to ignore it.*)

PHIL. C'mon Greg, tell us. Was it fun?

GREG. …It was ok.

PHIL. (*Acting more strange, than threatening, somewhat similar to* **JOAN**'s *cover up behavior in the opening scene.*) Just ok? C'mon, tell us more. I want to hear about it.

GREG. Are you ok, Phil?

PHIL. I'm fine. What's the big deal? You just screwed my wife in my bedroom. I just want you to share the experience with us. That's all.

GREG. I'd rather not.

PHIL. C'mon Greg, loosen up. Tonight is about sharing. So share!

GREG. I…I don't have anything to share.

(*He gets up and moves away from* **PHIL.**)

LISA. (*in response to* **GREG**'s *comment*) Uh oh!

GREG. What?

LISA. (*not wanting to go there*) Nothing.

GREG. Why did you say, "Uh oh"?

LISA. I don't know…I just…It was nothing.

GREG. No, it wasn't nothing. It was something.

LISA. It was nothing, Greg.

GREG. Why did you say, "Uh oh?"

LISA. I don't know, Greg. I just said it.

GREG. You think I couldn't do it.

(**LISA** *buries her head.* **GREG** *addresses the others.*)

She thinks I couldn't get it up.

LISA. I didn't say that.

GREG. Yeah, you did.

LISA. No, I didn't.

GREG. You're wrong.

LISA. Ok.

GREG. I did.

LISA. Fine.

GREG. No problem.

LISA. Great.

GREG. Rock of Gibraltar!

LISA. Greg!

GREG. To the ceiling and beyond!!

LISA. Oh, brother.

GREG. We did it two times, six different positions, all over the room!!!

(GREG flails around as he says this and finishes face to face with a stern looking PHIL.)

CARL. …Now that's what I call sharing.

GREG. Sorry, Phil. It wasn't directed at you.

(PHIL says nothing. They all sit quietly.)

KELLY. …I'm really feeling uncomfortable about this whole experience.

CARL. It's all right honey, everything's gonna be ok.

KELLY. Ok? A "major event" just happened here.

CARL. … "Cloning!" is a major event. This was sex, consensual sex. It's supposed to be fun.

KELLY. …Was it?

CARL. Fun?

(She waits for an answer.)

…Yes.

KELLY. Oh.

CARL. Are you jealous?

KELLY. Maybe.

CARL. Don't be. You're the one I want.

KELLY. *(looking around the room)* Could we discuss this somewhere else?

CARL. Ok. *(to the others)* Please excuse us.

(KELLY pulls him off to a bedroom.)

PHIL. *(to* **JOAN***)* Happy now?

JOAN. Huh?

PHIL. Are you happy that Carl and Kelly are arguing?

JOAN. No.

PHIL. Don't you think it's your fault?

JOAN. No, I don't.

PHIL. Did you have a good time tonight?

JOAN. *(straightforward)* Real good.

PHIL. Glad to hear it.

LISA. Is everything all right with you guys?

PHIL. It's no big deal.

LISA. What happened?

PHIL. Nothing happened.

JOAN. Yeah, but it would have, if I got home ten minutes later.

PHIL. Joan!

JOAN. I caught Phil with his girlfriend here this afternoon.

PHIL. You're gonna bring everybody into this?

JOAN. Privacy's just not in the air tonight.

PHIL. Ok, fine. Why don't we just run our whole marriage out there for everybody to see.

JOAN. Ok. Let's.

PHIL. Great, where do you want to start?

JOAN. We could start with your girlfriend.

PHIL. *(protesting, as if he's got a real point)* She's not my girlfriend. She's a hooker.

JOAN. *(fake sincerity)* Excuse me, my mistake.

(To **GREG** *and* **LISA***)*

I don't want to make my husband look bad.

(To **PHIL***)*

Tell everyone about the hooker.

PHIL. I don't think they want to hear about it.

LISA. I'd like to hear about it.

GREG. This is none of our business.

(He starts to get up but **JOAN** *immediately stops him.)*

JOAN. Sit down!

*(***GREG*** immediately sits.)*

C'mon, Phil. You're into sharing. Remember?

PHIL. *(blurts out)* All right! I was with her six times. Once a month, for the last six months. The exact same time that our sex life started improving.

JOAN. …What?

PHIL. We've had problems Joan, whether you want to acknowledge it or not. Having sex less than once a month does not constitute a marriage.

JOAN. I think I missed something.

PHIL. Did you know that one time last year, we went 56 days in a row without having sex? Did you know that?

JOAN. No, I wasn't aware.

PHIL. It's true, 56 days in a row.

GREG. Wow, one more day, you could'a broke Dimaggio's streak.

JOAN. I don't know what you're talking about, Phil. We've been doing it a lot more than once a month.

PHIL. Yes…ever since I started seeing the hooker.

*(***JOAN*** is speechless.)*

It brought me back to life. She woke me up. Which in turn, woke you up. The hooker made us want to have sex more often.

JOAN. Do you have her address? I want to send her a thank you card.

PHIL. It's true, Joan. We had no sex life. Husbands and wives are supposed to have sex. It's what they do.

JOAN. Is that the official way to determine the success of a marriage?

PHIL. Show me a couple that fucks a lot, and I'll show you a happy marriage.

(At that moment we suddenly hear moans of ecstacy coming from offstage. It starts faint but gradually builds.

The four of them just listen in disbelief. It goes on for about 20 or 30 seconds, then finally reaches a climax.)

GREG. Must be the happiest marriage in town.

PHIL. I don't believe this.

GREG. Do you think they're done?

PHIL. I don't think Carl's ever done.

GREG. I hope he doesn't go for me next.

LISA. I guess they're not arguing any more.

JOAN. Good for them.

PHIL Yeah, good for everybody. It's one big orgasm house. *(to* **JOAN***)* Remind me to take the W-E-L off our WELCOME mat.

(A few moments go by and then **KELLY** *and* **CARL** *emerge from the bedroom.* **KELLY** *comes out first, looking annoyed and walking away.* **CARL** *follows.)*

CARL. C'mon, Kel.

KELLY. Don't touch me.

CARL. Kelly.

KELLY. Don't even talk to me.

*(**CARL** just shakes his head in futility.)*

LISA. What happened?

KELLY. He does it every time.

LISA. What?

KELLY. Every single time.

LISA. What?

KELLY. Every time we disagree about something, he seduces me.

CARL. So?

KELLY. So, you're avoiding the problem.

CARL. I'm not avoiding anything. I just like to seduce you.

KELLY. It's manipulative.

CARL. It's fun.

KELLY. We never accomplish anything.

CARL. I thought we just accomplished a lot.

(KELLY shakes her head, not knowing what to say.)

JOAN. Kelly, if you didn't want to be seduced, why did you respond?

KELLY. I can't help it and he knows that.

CARL. Didn't you enjoy it?

KELLY. That's not the point.

CARL. Of course that's the point. That's the only point.

KELLY. You turn everything into sex. That's a problem.

CARL. I can't resist you and you can't resist me. *(sarcastically)* Boy, are we in trouble!

KELLY. We are if we keep avoiding things.

CARL. I'm not avoiding anything. You want to talk, let's talk.

(He motions toward the bedroom, where they just came from.)

KELLY. *(No way she's going off with him again.)* Until you make another move.

CARL. Don't worry. I'm out of commission for at least five minutes.

KELLY. Aren't you worried about what happened here? For all of us?

CARL. Worrying is what causes the problem.

PHIL. *(jumping in)* You know, Carl, sex isn't always good. Sometimes it's wrong.

JOAN. And when might those times be, honey?

PHIL. You're the one who made tonight happen. I think what you did here tonight is worse than what I did.

JOAN. *(surprised by that one)* What I did, is worse than what you did?

PHIL. What you did involves the lives and marriages of our friends. What I did is nothing more than glorified masturbation.

JOAN. Is that what it said in her ad? "Best glorified masturbation in town."

CARL. What are they talking about?

GREG. You missed a chapter.

CARL. Tell me.

GREG. Joan caught Phil with a hooker today.

JOAN. And Phil thinks it's nothing. Just a minor detail in a marriage.

PHIL. You know what's the single, most amazing thing on Earth?

GREG. That we're talking about this shit?

PHIL. No, that most women are more concerned what their husband does when he's not around, then what he does when he is. How do you explain that?

CARL. Good question.

KELLY. You were with another woman behind her back.

PHIL. And why are you so bothered by it?

JOAN. What?!

PHIL. I know it's an amazing question. But tell me. Why will people stick it out forever with a partner who's manipulative, selfish, controlling, and a million other things, but immediately break up with someone who cheats?

JOAN. Ever hear of a thing called the marriage vows?

PHIL. Yeah, but I didn't write them. I want to know what it means to you.

JOAN. It means you and me. That's what marriage is – a husband and wife together exclusively. That's why you get married.

PHIL. Really? I thought you get married because you're in love. I thought you get married because you want to share things and do things together. I thought you get married because you want to have a family. I never thought the number one reason for getting married was to prevent your partner from having an orgasm with someone else.

JOAN. I gotta give you credit for one thing.

PHIL. What?

JOAN. Out of all the husbands who've had affairs, you're probably the only one, who instead of spending all his time trying to cover it up, has devoted himself to defending it.

PHIL. No, I haven't.

JOAN. Yeah, you have. You were ready for this. You did it right here in our living room, when I was due home in a few hours. It's almost as if you wanted to get caught… Is that it? Did you want me to catch you?

(**PHIL** *just stares at her as there must be some truth to her question.*)

…Were we that bad off?

(**JOAN** *is processing all this as they continue to look at each other.*)

PHIL. …I just don't think it's the worst thing in the world.

LISA. Then why are you so bothered by the swap?

PHIL. Because I'm worried about everyone else.

CARL. *(brings his hand to his mouth and does a fake cough as he says…)* Bullshit!

PHIL. What?

LISA. I think you're jealous.

PHIL. So what if I am? A little jealousy can be a good thing.

CARL. A little jealousy is like a little poison. It's all toxic.

KELLY. *(to* **CARL***)* How about cheating? Is that ok?

CARL. Huh?

KELLY. Is cheating ok?

CARL. I don't know. Every situation's different.

KELLY. It's just sex, right?

CARL. *(wondering where she's headed)* I guess…

KELLY. How many times have you done it?

CARL. I haven't.

KELLY. Yeah, right.

CARL. I haven't.

KELLY. Why not? It's just sex. And sex is the most fun thing in the world, isn't it?

CARL. Because I don't want to lie to you.

KELLY. So cheating isn't so bad, but lying about it is?

CARL. Something like that.

KELLY. In that case I have something to tell you…I slept with my boss.

CARL. …Are you serious?

KELLY. Dead serious.

CARL. When?

KELLY. Last year.

CARL. …How was it?

KELLY. Good.

CARL. *(thinks for a moment)* …You still love me?

KELLY. Yes, of course.

CARL. Ok.

(As if the case is closed.)

KELLY. That's it?

CARL. That's it.

KELLY. You're not upset?

CARL. No.

PHIL. *(does the same fake cough as CARL just did)* Bullshit!

CARL. I'm not upset.

KELLY. What if I fell in love with him and wanted to leave you?

CARL. Then I'd be upset.

KELLY. Well it could have happened.

CARL. But it didn't.

KELLY. I lied to you. Do you care about that?

CARL. Why did you lie?

KELLY. Because I didn't want to hurt you.

CARL. *(in a loving and admiring way to KELLY)* Oh, honey, that's a good reason.

(KELLY looks around as if CARL is crazy.)

PHIL. But, according to you, you wouldn't have been hurt.

CARL. She didn't know that.

PHIL. So, she can sleep with anyone she wants and lie to you any time, as long as she has a good reason?

CARL. Yes, I trust her.

JOAN. How can you trust her? She cheated on you.

CARL. I trust that she's a good person and never acts with evil intentions. That's how I define trust. Not by who she has fun with when I'm not around.

LISA. Don't you want to know why she did it?

CARL. I think I know why.

KELLY. Why?

CARL. I think it's in your nature.

KELLY. What the hell do you mean by that?

CARL. You're free and uninhibited. You love sex, and that makes you sexy. I love it that everything turns you on, whatever it is, even if it's another man. You never hold anything back. Do you know how few women are like that?

KELLY. All I know is I've been feeling guilty about this for a year.

CARL. I'm ok.

(He gives her a hug. **KELLY** *allows it, but is holding back still looking puzzled.)*

LISA. ...I believe him Kelly.

GREG. *(sarcastically)* Well, that makes it official.

LISA. What did I do?

GREG. Forget it.

LISA. You know Greg, every once in a while, in life, it's ok to say what's on your mind.

GREG. A little difference between saying what's on your mind and controlling everything.

LISA. I said I believed him. How is that controlling?

GREG. *(gets up and moves away from her)* Nevermind. It's just a style you've got.

LISA. This is coming from a guy who can't even make dinner plans without having a war inside his head.

GREG. What are you talking about?

LISA. *(mocking him)* "Lisa, what do you want to eat tonight? I...I thought about Chinese food, but if you'd rather have Italian, that's ok. Well, well actually, we don't even have to go out if you don't want to. Um, um, we could make something in the house if you prefer. Or then again, we, we, we could pick up fast food...I mean we got all kinds of options. I'm totally open...So what, what, what do you think?"

GREG. You're putting me down for being considerate?

LISA. I'm putting you down because you can't take charge of anything. Just once in your life I'd like to hear you say something like, "Lisa, we're having Chinese food tonight. Be ready at seven."

GREG. So I should try it your way and tell you what to do every second of every day?

LISA. Is that what you think I do?

GREG. Yeah, but don't worry about it, it's very pleasant. *(mocking)* "Don't take the freeway, take the streets. Don't wear this shirt, wear that shirt. Don't fuck me this way, fuck me that way."

(As he says the last one, he acts it out by thrusting in different directions.)

I can't even breathe without checking with you to see if I did it right. Wait a minute. How's this?

(He takes one slow, deliberate, stressed out breath.)

Was that ok?

KELLY. *(The masseuse jumping in)* Actually it was all up here.

(pointing to her chest)

It should be down here.

(pointing to her belly, then looking embarrassed for interrupting)

GREG. And it's not just telling me what to do. It's constantly making little comments to try to make me feel bad.

LISA. I don't know what you're talking about.

GREG. It's true. You do it all the time. Any time I'm having fun or feeling good about myself, you find a way to put me down.

LISA. I do not.

GREG. Yeah you do. All the time.

LISA. Really? Like when, Greg? Give me an example.

GREG. *(As he hears* **LISA***'s request, a wonderfully fulfilled smile suddenly comes over his face)* ...Ok, I will.

(He walks over to his jacket, pulls a small notebook out of his pocket, and proudly starts reading from it. He savors every sentence, as he has been waiting a long time for this moment.)

March 24! At Matthew's birthday party, right after we all finished singing "Happy Birthday", you said to me, and I quote, *(He now looks up at her and imitates the way she must have done it.)* "Honey, next time could you just lip sync it."

(back to notebook)

May 17th, on our trip to Six Flags, when Olivia said, "Mommy, I'm afraid of the rides." You replied, *(imitating again)* "Don't worry baby, they can't be any scarier than Daddy's driving."

(notebook again)

June 16th, when I came charging in the house to tell you I got a raise, you said, *(one more imitation)* "Wow! Maybe someday you'll make as much as me."

(notebook)

July 20th, when I took my shirt off at the beach...

LISA. *(cutting him off)* You write these things down?

GREG. *(as if it's completely normal)* Yep.

(continues)

July 20th, at the beach...

LISA. I don't want to hear it.

GREG. You sure? It was one of your better ones.

LISA. *(dumbfounded)* ...What possessed you to write this stuff down?

GREG. *(triumphantly exploding like he just scored the winning touchdown in the Superbowl)* Because I knew this day was coming!!!!!!!!.... I knew, sure as I'm alive, that one day we would be out somewhere, arguing over how you constantly put me down, and that you would very calmly and very confidently look me straight in the eye and say, "Like when, Greg? Give me an example." And I didn't want to be unprepared!!!!!!

LISA. You're sick.

GREG. Oh, *I'm* sick?

LISA. You hold everything in and count it against me, bit by bit. It's like a secret boxing match. You got me on a scorecard where you keep deducting points every time I do something you don't like, but you don't tell me about it. It's like I'm being knocked out of the ring and I don't even know I'm getting hit.

GREG. What am I supposed to do? If I point out every single thing, we'll be fighting all the time.

LISA. Pick your battles and speak up. That's all. And the rest of the time let it go. You don't have to fall apart over every comment I make.

GREG. I'm not falling apart. It's just...do you know, that out of all the people in my life, you're the only one who ever tries to stop me from being happy?

LISA. *(Slightly hurt, she takes it in for a minute.)* ...No, I didn't know that.

GREG. The only one.

JOAN. ...She let you have a happy time tonight.

(The others look at her. **JOAN** *now shakes her head, embarrassed by her interruption.)*

GREG. Cause it suited her. She had one too. Everyone had a good time tonight.

PHIL. Not everyone.

*(Everyone turns and looks surprised at **PHIL**'s comment.)*

CARL. ...Honey, I think you were just insulted.

PHIL. We didn't do it.

CARL. ...Was there a problem with "Phil Junior?"

PHIL. It didn't feel right.

JOAN. *(To **PHIL**)* It didn't feel right?

PHIL. No, it didn't.

JOAN. Funny, isn't it?

PHIL. What?

JOAN. You would spend our money, to do it with a stranger, behind my back, but you wouldn't do it for free, with someone you know and like, when you obviously had my permission. Don't you think that's funny?

PHIL. I explained it already.

JOAN. *(nodding)* Glorified masturbation.

PHIL. We need to work on things.

JOAN. How come after a man gets caught cheating, it's always the time he wants to work the hardest on the relationship?

PHIL. How come you don't want to work on it?

JOAN. We're having a party. I don't want to work. I want to play.

PHIL. Look at you. You're enraged, but you won't show it.

JOAN. Actually, I feel pretty good.

PHIL. You're angry, Joan, and you need to talk about it.

JOAN. I don't want to. There was something very liberating about tonight and at the moment I just want to think about that.

*(**PHIL** just stares at **JOAN**.)*

GREG. *(meanwhile, still perusing his notebook)* ...August 22nd, at the post office...

(He looks up and then stifles himself.)

LISA. *(stares at **GREG**)* ...Is it that bad?

GREG. Let's discuss it later.

(He puts the notebook in his pocket.)

LISA. Discuss what?

GREG. Nothing, it can wait till tomorrow.

LISA. What can wait till tomorrow?

GREG. You really want me to tell you?

LISA. *(sarcastically)* No, I'd rather guess.

GREG. Tonight.

LISA. What about tonight?

GREG. Why don't we finish this at home?

LISA. *(persisting)* What about tonight?

(No response.)

Are you sure you got it up?

GREG. Thru the roof.

LISA. Then what?

GREG. That! That's the point. With her, I was a stud!

*(As he says that, he accidently exchanges an uncomfortable glance with **PHIL**.)*

…Sorry, Phil.

*(back to **LISA**)* With you I strike out half the time.

LISA. With her, you had no pressure. With me, you got notebooks. You do it to yourself.

GREG. I do it?

LISA. Ok, we both do it. Either way, it's all up here. *(pointing to her head)*

GREG. *(realization)* …I want more.

LISA. Ok, you can have more.

GREG. No, I mean tonight. I want to do this again.

LISA. *(smiles)* Be happy you did it once.

GREG. I am. Now I want twice.

PHIL. *(jumping in)* Can I interject here?

LISA. We can talk about it later.

GREG. You wanted to talk. Let's talk. I want more.

LISA. Take it easy.

GREG. No. I want more. And I'm gonna get more! I'm not sure how or where, but I'm getting it…Another swap, an orgy… *(His eyes fall on* **PHIL.***)* Maybe one of Phil's hookers.

(Poor **PHIL** *again looks troubled.)*

I don't know, but I want more!

LISA. That's enough, Greg.

GREG. No, that's the point. It's not enough. All these years, it's never been enough. I want other women.

LISA. You can't have them.

GREG. I can have whatever I want. You're not telling me what to do anymore.

LISA. We're married. That's not the deal.

GREG. Deals change.

LISA. You can't have me and other women.

GREG. I did tonight.

LISA. Special case.

GREG. I want a new deal.

LISA. You can't have one.

GREG. I want one.

LISA. So it's all about you?

GREG. Why not? For 15 years it's been all about you.

LISA. Oh really, it's all about me? I guess that's why I'm the one who plans all the birthday parties. And that's why I'm the one who buys all the Christmas presents. And that's why I do all the shopping. And I buy all the clothes. Because it's all about me.

GREG. I do just as much as you do.

LISA. Bullshit! If it wasn't for me, your kids would be walking around naked. You never step up! You never take charge! I do everything!

GREG. Really? Who coaches all their baseball teams? Who takes them to the park all the time and practices with them for hours and hours?

LISA. Those things don't count.

GREG. What?!

LISA. They don't count.

GREG. Why not?

LISA. Because you enjoy them.

GREG. *(blown away)* You're telling me that none of the sports stuff that I do with the kids counts, because I enjoy it?

LISA. Yes.

GREG. *(digests it for a moment, then reaches into his pocket, pulls out the notebook, and starts writing.)* ...Sports don't count.

LISA. *(grabs the notebook out of his hand and throws it across the room)* That's enough!

CARL. Mellow out people. You're taking life too seriously.

KELLY. *(disturbed by **CARL**'s carefree attitude)* Carl!

CARL. *(innocently)* What?

KELLY. *(shaking her head)* Nothing affects you, does it? You just laugh off everything.

CARL. No, I don't.

KELLY. Yes, you do. Are you capable of getting upset? Does anything really matter to you? Our home? Your career? Brian? Do you care about him?

CARL. *(looks at her like she's crazy)* Oh, Kelly. I'd give my life 100 times over for our son. There isn't anything on Earth that I wouldn't do for him. And you know it. C'mon, just because I'm horny, you think that there's anything on this planet that matters to me, even one tenth as much as his well being?

KELLY. Sometimes it's hard to tell with you.

CARL. That's the kind of thinking that causes all the problems, not mine.

JOAN. I think man's obsessive desire for sex causes a few of the problems.

CARL. No, it's the stifling of that desire. That's the trouble. I'm telling you, if society stifled man's desire to eat, it would be the same thing.

JOAN. We need food to survive.

CARL. Not good food. We don't need good tasting food to survive. I'm telling you, if that desire was stifled, the way sex is, instead of trying to meet women, men would spend all their time trying to meet chefs.

GREG. Do you spend all your time thinking about this shit?

CARL. I just think everybody's got it backwards.

KELLY. What about love?

CARL. What about it?

KELLY. I don't know. I guess I'm still a little confused. I love you, but I had sex with someone else behind your back and I enjoyed it. And you say you love me, but you don't even mind that I did it. Doesn't that seem a little backwards to you?

CARL. No, it seems like sanity to me.

KELLY. You're unbelievable.

CARL. Why?

KELLY. I had an affair with my boss. He charmed me, he seduced me, he made love to me, and I liked it. It should bother you!

CARL. How does it prove anything if I get upset?

KELLY. It would prove that you care.

CARL. Do you honestly doubt that? Married eleven years, and I still can't keep my hands off of you.

KELLY. Sex.

CARL. Not sex, you. Men are horny animals and I'm the leader of the pack. We'll sleep with women we've never met. We'll sleep with women we don't even like.

(As he says that, his eyes fall on **LISA.** *He shakes his head and gestures to indicate that he doesn't mean her, as a woman he doesn't like.* **LISA** *just shakes her head as if he's ridiculous.)*

But we can't stay hot about the same person for 11 years unless we think they're special, inside and out. Nobody can do that, not even me.

KELLY. But it's more than that. I want a man who needs me. I want a man who will fight for me. Like tonight, I walked off with Phil right in front of you and you did nothing.

CARL. What do you want me to do, beat him up?

KELLY. *(without really thinking about it)* Yes.

(PHIL hears that and chuckles at the absurdity of it.)

CARL. *(after a few moments)* ...Ok.

(CARL makes a sudden move toward PHIL. PHIL jumps up looking alarmed.)

KELLY. No, stop!

(She steps in front of CARL. Everyone is startled. CARL walks away.)

PHIL. *(several moments later, when the threat is over)* ...What the fuck?!!!

KELLY. *(going to CARL)* Were you really going to beat him up?

CARL. *(like it's obvious)* No...But, I'll do whatever I have to for you.

KELLY. What if I really fell in love with my boss and left you forever? Then what would you do?

CARL. ...I'd die.

KELLY. What?

CARL. If you left me forever, I'd die.

KELLY. Then how can you flirt with it?

CARL. Because that's who I am. That's how I see the world. You excite me. You thrill me. And you put up with me. In every way, you are the perfect woman for me. And I need you more than you'll ever know. I loved you the first second I saw you and I always will.

(KELLY takes it all in. They kiss.)

GREG. I'm not sure I like him when he's sincere.

JOAN. I like him.

PHIL. You want to sleep with him, too?

JOAN. Yeah, I would.

CARL. *(breaking away from* **KELLY***)* Trifecta!

(He jokingly steps toward **JOAN** *as if he will now get to have sex with her.* **KELLY** *grabs him and playfully smacks him.)*

PHIL. When are you gonna let it out?

JOAN. Let what out?

PHIL. What you're really feeling.

JOAN. I told you, I'm feeling good.

PHIL. Don't sweep it under the rug.

JOAN. Maybe it's you, who's doing the sweeping.

PHIL. I'll talk about anything, whatever it is, and you know that.

JOAN. That's right, Phil. You pretend you're a lawyer, make your case and you think you've done something. Why do you think that whoever strings together the best group of sentences must be right? Yes Phil, you'll talk about anything. No question about it. Your words never get swept away. It's you heart that's under the rug.

PHIL. How can you expect my heart, if you won't talk to me?

JOAN. How come you're so much better with customers than with me?

PHIL. What?

JOAN. I've seen you. You're good. You're the best. You can get anything out of a customer. You charm them to death. Why can't you do that with me?

PHIL. This isn't business.

JOAN. No, it isn't. You're better at that.

PHIL. *(sarcastic)* Thanks.

JOAN. You used to do it. In the beginning…Talk about sweeping. Every time I saw you, you swept me right off my feet. You brought me flowers, you took me dancing, you made me laugh. You used to charm me all the time. Do you remember?

PHIL. *(nods)* ...You used to do a "certain thing" to me all the time. Do you remember?

(**JOAN** *cracks half a smile with embarrassment then nods.*)

Things change, I guess.

JOAN. ...You want me to do it now?

PHIL. What?

JOAN. That certain thing.

PHIL. Huh?

JOAN. Do you want me to do it now?

PHIL. What are you doing?

JOAN. I'm offering you a blow job. Do you want it?

PHIL. What? I don't get it.

JOAN. There's nothing to get. It's a simple question.

(**PHIL** *is not sure what to do. He looks around at the others and sees* **CARL** *smiling and nodding with approval.*)

GREG. *(jumping in)* She's good.

(**GREG** *quickly buries his face, mortified that those words just came out of his mouth.* **JOAN** *turns and looks at* **GREG**, *a little shocked and embarrassed.*)

(*A moment later, as if to call her bluff,* **PHIL** *goes and sits in a bar stool with his legs open and ready for her.*)

PHIL. Ok, let's have it, c'mon.

(*She comes over and kneels down in front of him.* **PHIL** *just laughs, confident that she won't go through with it.*)

CARL. Excuse me, honey.

(**CARL** *now moves past* **KELLY** *to the arm of the couch, to get a bird's eye view.* **KELLY** *shakes her head at her crazy husband.*)

(*Meanwhile,* **JOAN** *starts to undo* **PHIL**'s *belt and then open his pants. Just as she's about to take it out,* **PHIL** *finally stops her and pulls away.*)

PHIL. What are you doing?!

JOAN. Isn't your penis still between your legs?

(He gets up and walks away annoyed.)

PHIL. All right Joan, that's enough. You know…It's unbelievable. You're so pissed off and you can't admit it, so you gotta fuck with me.

JOAN. I'm not fucking with you. I was gonna give you a blow job.

PHIL. Right here, right now? In front of everyone?

(She takes a good look around the room.)

JOAN. …At this point, I couldn't faze anybody…We can do it in the bedroom if you want.

PHIL. I don't want it.

JOAN. Ok.

(JOAN looks rejected. There is silence for a few seconds.)

CARL. *(finally)* …I'll take it.

(CARL gets up, goes to the same stool PHIL sat in, pulls down his pants exposing his underwear, and sits with a big grin on his face. KELLY comes over, slaps him in the back of the head, and drags him back to the couch. CARL puts on an innocent, "What did I do?" look. They have a several second exchange as if KELLY is the parent and CARL is the naughty, but innocent looking child.)

PHIL. *(After CARL and KELLY have settled)* *(To JOAN)* Always playing games.

JOAN. It's not a game. I just had an impulse, to please you. Just for the hell of it. Isn't that the way it's supposed to be?

PHIL. *(sarcastic)* So everything's fine and we're gonna live happily ever after?

JOAN. Sure, why not.

PHIL. Enough with the bullshit, Joan. You can never stop with all the bullshit.

JOAN. *(turning serious)* I walk in to find you half naked with some slut in our living room and this is bullshit?

PHIL. No, but why is cheating automatically the worst thing that can happen in a marriage?

JOAN. Because it is!

PHIL. Oh, but it's ok to shut down and bury everything inside and hold on to it forever, and ever and ever and ever….

JOAN. *(exploding)* Yes it is!! You cheated on me!! You broke my heart!!

PHIL. It was one night, ten years ago! And I've apologized for it a thousand times. And I've devoted myself to you every day since. But you just won't let it go.

JOAN. Because I could never trust you after that. And now you did it again.

PHIL. Yes, but you know what? At least we're finally talking about it.

JOAN. Oh, is that why you brought a hooker here? For us?

PHIL. There is no "us", Joan. "Us" ended years ago because you could never forgive me.

(He takes a breath, then he puts his hands on her arms and addresses her sincerely.)

…I love you Joan. And for the last time, I'm sorry.

(He repeats it slowly, sincerely, and emphatically right in her eyes)

I…am…sorry! But I won't live this way any more. Either forgive me or leave me.

(He walks away. **JOAN** *just takes it in. She is clearly affected by what he said. There is silence for several moments.)*

LISA. *(To* **GREG***)* …Greg, what about us?

GREG. You tell me.

LISA. No, you tell me.

GREG. I'm doing what I want, whenever I want. You're free to do the same.

LISA. So it's all about you again?

(He gives her a hug. **JOAN** *looks uncomfortable. Then he turns toward* **PHIL**.*)*

GREG. *(cont.)* Phil…I love what you've done with the bedroom.

*(***GREG*** shakes his head feeling stupid about that comment. He exits.* **LISA**, *almost in tears, follows him a moment later.* **JOAN** *tries to stop* **LISA**, *but she can't. Many seconds go by, as the others just take it all in.)*

CARL. *(finally)* …You think they'll take the streets or the freeway?

PHIL. This is our fault.

CARL. It's not anybody's fault.

PHIL. If tonight didn't happen…

CARL. Their marriage obviously had troubles before tonight.

JOAN. Every marriage has some troubles. But when you add something like this to the list…

CARL. Something like what? Look, I don't like what just happened with them, and I understand that this wasn't exactly a typical evening, but the Earth didn't move off its axis tonight.

PHIL. All right Carl, you can down play anything. But they gotta deal with this.

CARL. Deal with what?

PHIL. *(amazed at Carl's attitude)* Why do I bother?

CARL. Nothing changed tonight. If anything it just uncovered what was already there, for all of us. People have desires, people have fantasies…Boy, wouldn't it be nice if you could have fantasies and actually tell your partner about them, without them getting all insecure and crazy? Wouldn't it be even nicer if you could live some of them out, and then come back and discuss it with the person you love the most? Wouldn't it be nice if sex actually helped more marriages than it hurt?

PHIL. …Wouldn't it be nice if you took your medication?

*(***CARL*** laughs.)*

GREG. No, this is about you. In fact, here, let me be the [guy] you're looking for. How's this?

(with authority)

Next Saturday night, Chinese food, 7:00, be ready. Swingers party at 9.

LISA. Is this a joke?

GREG. Nope.

LISA. You feel like a big man now?

GREG. I feel good.

(LISA digests the moment. After a few seconds, she changes gears, and now looks admiringly at GREG's sudden show of strength)

LISA. Finally standing up to me, huh?

GREG. Yep.

(She walks over to him and puts her arms around him seductively. GREG unsure how to react, is distant at first, but gradually starts softening, and puts his arms around her.)

LISA. You know, maybe if you acted like this more of[ten] we'd have a better marriage.

GREG. *(In disbelief that she's doing it again, he throws his [hands] up in the air.)* I'm done.

LISA. What do you mean?

GREG. I'm tired of being beaten up because I'm no[t the] guy you want me to be. I'm done.

LISA. *(not expecting that)* What are you talking about?

GREG. It's over, Lisa.

(He tries to walk away from her, but she grabs him.)

LISA. *(appealing to him)* But Greg I love you. I'm sorry.

GREG. *(He takes her in for a moment.)* ...You know may[be if] you acted like this more often, we'd still HAVE a [mar]riage.

(He walks away from her, grabs his jacket and goes t[o] JOAN.)

Joan, thank you.

CARL. Tonight, Kelly told me she slept with her boss, and I just had sex with another woman, and I feel even closer to her than before. I guess I must be insane.

JOAN. What about you, Kelly? You feel the same way?

KELLY. Yeah, I feel he's insane…

(**KELLY** *and* **CARL** *smile at each other.*)

He wants me to be happy, no matter what I do and he trusts me, no matter what I do. I think if he woke up in the middle of the night and saw me standing over him with a knife, he'd say, "I love you," roll over, and go back to sleep. He would automatically know that I wasn't there to hurt him. I don't know anyone else who thinks the way he does.

(*They both look lovingly at each other. They start to kiss. It quickly gets hot and heavy and they start groping each other.*)

PHIL. (*in disbelief*) Seriously?

(**CARL** *is really getting into it.* **KELLY** *taps* **CARL** *on the shoulder indicating that the others are watching.* **CARL** *snaps out of it.*)

KELLY. …I think it's getting late.

(*They quickly gather themselves and head to the door. They are anxious to be alone. Right before leaving,* **CARL** *looks back.*)

CARL. Best get-together yet.

(*They exit.*)

JOAN. …You think they're gonna go home and do it again?

PHIL. (*shakes his head*) No…too long to wait. They'll probably do it in our yard.

(*They share a laugh. Then several seconds go by as they have a quiet and awkward moment suddenly being alone with each other.* **JOAN** *goes and sits in a bar stool.* **PHIL** *studies her for a few moments. He finally gets up, goes to the stereo, picks up the remote control, and puts a* *romantic song on. Then he walks over and takes a flower from the vase. He gradually makes his way over to* **JOAN** *with a playful smile and a little dance in his step. He is trying to be cute and make her laugh. He hands her the flower in a gentlemanly way. Then he leads her off the stool and starts slow dancing with her.* **JOAN** *is guarded at first, but gradually becomes more comfortable. They embrace. Now* **JOAN** *takes over and maneuvers* **PHIL** *toward the same bar stool as he sat in before. She sits him on it. She gives him a warm kiss on the lips. Then she gradually works her way down his body to his waist. As she starts to move her head just a little below his waist,* **PHIL** *ecstatically looks to the sky and the lights fade out.)*

THE END

OTHER TITLES AVAILABLE FROM SAMUEL FRENCH

A NIGHT IN PROVENCE

Robin Hawdon

Comedy / 3m, 3f

From the author of *Don't Dress for Dinner!*

Ah Provence! The French Riviera. Where the well-to-do rent luxury villas for exorbitant sums in order to get their annual fix of sun, sea, and haute cuisine. However, imagine the crisis if one such sumptuous place was double booked. Worse – imagine it triple booked! By a French couple, an English couple, and heaven forbid, an Irish/American couple. Marriages have foundered on less. Add the ingredients of copious champagne, heightened sexual impulses, and ingrained cultural differences, and the European Union could well implode!

The USA and Europe have seen many comedies by Robin Hawdon, but none to threaten international relations on this scale. "…Now this admirable dinner theatre is reducing audiences to helpless laughter once more with this consistently entertaining playwright's latest work…makes for a great night out."
–*Oxford Times*

"Chaos, banter, and sexually charged jokes ensue when three couples clash at a holiday villa in Provence…This fast-paced romp was a joy to watch from start to finish…A wonderful way to spice up a chilly evening."
–*Wokingham Times*

"An overcrowded French holiday villa makes for a houseful of laughs…Robin Hawdon keeps the sexual frisson simmering in one of the Mill's unqualified successes…"
–*Reading Evening Post*

SAMUELFRENCH.COM

OTHER TITLES AVAILABLE FROM SAMUEL FRENCH

LOVES AND HOURS

Stephen Metcalfe

Comedy / 4m, 4f, with doubling / Multiple sets

Love. Age. Perspective. The wisdom learned of experience. The innocence and impatience of youth. Thrills. Romance. Movies, wine, antiques and rock and roll. *Loves & Hours* is the story of Dan Tilney; newly divorced, empty nester, and a man now totally at a loss as to what to do with the rest of his life. His friends know. Dan needs a girl. But will it be Charlotte, beautiful, bursting with life and twenty years his junior? Or will it be Julia; his life long friend and confidant. And what about his teenage son who is having an affair with a neighbor? And his ex-wife who has announced she's gay? What about his best friend, Harold,—who is going through a mid-life crisis and his daughter, Rebecca, who is seemingly furious with everything and everyone. In this gentle comedy, life and love are complicated for young and not so young alike.

OTHER TITLES AVAILABLE FROM SAMUEL FRENCH

FOR BETTER

Eric Coble

3m, 3f / Comedy

In this plugged-in world of email, text-messaging and camera phones, do a bride and groom really need to be in the same country to go on a honeymoon? Karen and Max are getting married. At least, if their jobs will ever let them be in the same city at the same time. A romantic comedy for the digital age, *For Better* is a hilarious new farce that pokes fun at our overdependence on the gadgets in our lives.

"Eric Coble's hilariously funny, psychologically astute portraits hit home with rib-tickling acuity"
– *The New York Times*

"Coble's work is a tour de force with physical and verbal comedy to spare"
– *The New Yorker*

"A Playwright to Watch: An unqualified original with rich and idiosyncratic works A spirit of playful invention pervades Coble's repertoire."
– *American Theatre Magazine*

"Coble's comedies are, of all things, genuinely funny"
– *Newsday*

SAMUELFRENCH.COM

OTHER TITLES AVAILABLE FROM SAMUEL FRENCH

YOU'VE GOT HATE MAIL

Billy Van Zandt and Jane Milmore

Comedy / 2m, 3f / Unit Set

"LOL! An audience is guaranteed to do just that" at this hilarious broadband comedy of errors. *You've Got Hate Mail* is Billy Van Zandt and Jane Milmore's comic answer to A.R. Gurney's *Love Letters*. In *You've Got Hate Mail*, love "bytes" all when an extra-marital affair goes horribly wrong, thanks to a juicy e-mail left sitting on a desktop. The story is told entirely in e-mails from laptop computers, although the play still manages to have an unforgettable chase scene — thanks to Blackberries and iPhones. The heartiest laugh-for-laugh show of all the Van Zandt-Milmore comedies.

"Outright guffaws greeted this 75-minute, intermissionless free-for-all!"
– Peter Filichia, *The Newark Star Ledger*

"Composed entirely of e-mails and text messages riotously enacted by a five-person ensemble, it may encourage you to keep your Black-Berry under lock and key."
– *New York Post*

"A funny play where the verbal zingers fly fast and furious!"
– Tom Chesek, *Asbury Park Press*

SAMUELFRENCH.COM

OTHER TITLES AVAILABLE FROM SAMUEL FRENCH

THE MAKEOVER

Patsy Hester Daussat

Comedy / 4m, 4f, 1m or f / Interior Set

It's a typical Saturday evening, as Mike and Melanie play games with their best friends, Victor and Paula. They have been neighbors for years, and each have a son home from college for the summer. Little does Melanie know that her happy, comfortable world will soon be thrown into turmoil. Mike has sent a letter to Facing Facts, Melanie and Paula's favorite reality television show. He believes Melanie, who has gained weight over the years, would be thrilled to have a makeover at Facing Facts' fabulous spa. After all, she and Paula rave about it. Unfortunately, every Monday night when Melanie and Paula watch the show, their husbands leave to play baseball. Poor Mike is clueless about the show's cruel, ratings-hungry hostess, Frances Montgomery, who thrives on humiliating those who are ambushed on the show. When the Facing Facts crew descends at her door, Melanie endures a disastrous ambush. Afterward, she cannot understand why Mike would subject her to national humiliation. Melanie tells him to be out of the house when she returns from the spa. Mike is hopeful that she will change her mind, but things only get worse the evening Melanie returns. Frances not only belittles Melanie again, she sets her sights on an oblivious Mike. Melanie finally explodes, throwing the Facing Facts crew out of her house, along with Mike. Events in the days that follow bring Melanie to realizations about herself and the important things in life.

"The new comedy-drama *The Makeover* is satisfying…and highly pleasurable…Daussat's play is quite entertaining and she earns a solid, robust share of laughs from her writing. Issues of being overweight in this country are presented…with brutal honesty, never once sounding preachy or whining, but instead with a truthful, immensely heartfelt observation…Daussat's talents are shown to be off to a great start…a solid audience pleaser…a knockout hit."
– *Talkin' Broadway*

SAMUELFRENCH.COM

www.ingramcontent.com/pod-product-compliance
Lightning Source LLC
Chambersburg PA
CBHW070649300426
44111CB00013B/2337